Behavioral Economics for Skeptics

HUGH SCHWARTZ

Alexandria, Virginia

Library of Congress Control Number: 2015915798
Hugh Schwartz, Alexandria, VA

Behavioral Economics for Skeptics

Hugh Schwartz, Alexandria, VA
hughschwar@aol.com

Rationality generally wins out in the long run and those who take rational positions are vindicated—not only in the stock market but in life in general. There are exceptions, of course, and some of them are fairly disturbing—such as the Money Illusion, the failure to allow (completely) for the gradual loss of purchasing power by currencies that do not undergo rapid inflation—but, by and large, rationality wins the day. Why, then, modify the behavioral assumptions of our financial and economic analysis—basically, the assumption that we try to do the best possible and those that are the most successful among us, achieve that?

The answer is that for many purposes we live from day to day and all-too-many of our decisions depend upon what happens in the short run, and rationality does not always triumph in the short run. Indeed, complete rationality does not always win out even in the long run.

The obligation, then, is not only to take account of the behavioral assumptions that are relevant for all periods of time, but to note, where there are deviations from rationality, the extent of those deviations. Behavioral economics has been very successful in detecting deviations from rationality, but much less concerned with dealing with the frequency of the deviations, and the approach has been disinclined to estimate either the cost of the various deviations or even the circumstances in which the deviations from rationality are overcome—such as the near end of the so-called January Effect, whereby stocks of smaller companies rose more in January than in other months, and the apparent tapering off of the so-called Winners' Curse by which those who win competitive bids to pay too much.

This inquiry into Behavioral Economics outlines what the approach has contributed and attempts to indicate where it needs to do more, even in a microeconomic context, if it is to be used more consistently by decision makers. For those who have always associated economics with supply and demand, note that behavioral economics is an effort to deal with supply and demand in the real world, where individuals do not always attempt to calculate what is mathematically optimal, and, indeed, where such an approach is not always feasible because there are just too many factors to be considered—and there is too much uncertainty.

What follows is a modified version of what was presented in the first half of an intensive course, offered in November 2014 in the University of the Republic in Uruguay. It incorporates several comments of Martín Egozcue, who taught the second half of the course, along with several of those of Simón Teitel, an economist who is at least somewhat skeptical of the approach. In addition, I have tried to take account of a number of suggestions of Stephen Schwartz, representing concerns of an individual who is not an economist. Several of the changes introduced in the first revision reflect reactions of Roy Lyford-Pike, an engineer who has worked in technical and managerial positions for major companies in the United States, Brazil and Uruguay. This second edition introduces a number of changes and additions throughout the presentation, along with two major considerations. First, and most important, it emphasizes the simultaneous development of two seemingly contradictory trends, the increasing acceptance of behavioral economics based on largely emotion-free experimental economics, and, the other, the increasing emphasis on the emotional content of so many of the heuristics or rules of thumb used in everyday decision making. In addition, this edition, as the earlier reprinting, notes the important work of Alvin Roth and colleagues in using behavioral economics to improve the initial allocation of kidney transplants and a number of other human placements that have been regarded as unsatisfactory.

CONTENTS

1

INTRODUCTION

Behavioral Economics might seem like a redundant name. Doesn't economics deal with human behavior in economic affairs generally, after all?

Unfortunately, the expression is not redundant.

A simplification of models is inevitable in any subject. That is the way of scientific advance. Yet, despite Einstein's advice to keep things as simple as possible, as that most distinguished scientist also cautioned, complex matters should not ignore complexities; often, one cannot solve a problem with the same type of thinking as that which created it.

Economics has been based, for some time, on models that assume optimization and maximization or very nearly that. Rationality has been the byword. That has certainly been true of what academics refer to as positive economics, but it also has been true for traditional economics' view of everyday descriptive economics in that it has been assumed that those who survived the travails of competition have optimized and maximized, or at least have come closer to optimization than most others. That may still leave them quite far from optimization, however.

Mainstream economic theory has had a normative presumption; it has assumed that people tend to behave in the manner that leads to the most efficient solutions, as economic theory demonstrates. It is not that economists have been so naïve as to ignore other considerations (which, they concede, may lead to different conclusions in individual cases). Nor is it that they believe that even surviving business enterprises seek only to do the best possible and are able to achieve that objective, but, as Nobel Laureate Milton Friedman wrote, economists have generally assumed that successful economic actors behave *as if* they were optimizing. Models along those lines have explained a great deal, and the errors of some actors in one direction are offset by compensating errors of others—though leading figures in the profession have denied that it is possible to predict anything on the basis of individual mistakes. Moreover, competitive markets tend to limit deviations from optimizing behavior. Nonetheless, those optimizing models miss something, and what they miss can help us understand the present better, and often help us predict better, improving the way in which we cope with the future. Note that it is not uncommon that those who proclaim economic rationality as a guiding principle, make other (often idiosyncratic) assumptions about human behavior when it comes to individual cases, particularly when they are called in as advisors or consultants.

Behavioral economics is descriptive; it deals with what transpires in the real world, and as such it introduces assumptions of human behavior that often differ from those of traditional economic theory. At times it reveals that the behavioral assumptions of human activity turn out to be precisely as economists have long maintained (particularly in the long run), but, more frequently, it shows that human behavior draws on factors revealed by the discipline of psychology and on matters of a sociological, cultural and political nature—even on neurological factors—and that these lead to deviations from rationality, certainly rationality in the restricted sense of mainstream economics.

Most economists' assumptions about human rationality have continued to hold despite the increasing availability of more data, the advances in models to cope with so much data, and an improvement in measurement techniques. All this attests to the shortcomings of the assumptions of rationality. Despite our frequent use of the words, maximization and optimization—in professional writings as well as in everyday conversation—the fact is that some problems do not lend themselves to optimization (certainly not in the time a decision must be made), that objectives other than optimization for the decision making unit often are involved (influenced by prevailing cultural attitudes and social interaction), and that there are limits to the willpower of people to do what they say they set out to do. For those reasons, traditional economic models often lack adequate guidance on how better to manage matters, particularly for changing circumstances such as those frequently unknowable ones that the future brings.

Is it any wonder that most economists were so taken by surprise by the magnitude of the financial and economic collapse of recent years—and that they have had so little of help to offer the world since then (indeed, that they continue to grope with alternative incentives and their timing in an effort to bring us out of the economic doldrums)? Even behavioral economists, most of whom are micro-oriented, have had little to say that has proved very useful in dealing with the larger picture.

This paper emphasizes the main thrusts of behavioral economics, the inclination of individuals, companies and other entities to replace careful calculation with heuristics or rules of thumb. It deals with applications such as those in finance (behavioral finance) and public policy ("nudging" for example, to get economic agents to do what is more in their interest). Implicit in the presentation is that the essence of behavioral economics has little to do with mathematics—which is not to deny that many of the proofs of behavioral economics rest on use of that tool. Note that the discussion of nudging and some of the latest uses of the behavioral approach, transforms behavioral economics into something more than simply a better description of what economic actors do and have done.

Many of the contributions of behavioral economics have been around for years, but were not taken seriously by the economics profession until they were shown to be more than anecdotal—by experiments, in the laboratory, at first, and then, in the field. Unfortunately, there still has been little effort to indicate which of the behavioral anomalies are widespread, which are relatively common, and which simply reflect exceptional circumstances, Nor have there been, until recently, efforts to indicate which are relatively easy to overcome by changes in public and private default mechanisms, minor changes in institutional arrangements and similarly small changes in government policy. This is another way of saying that there has not been much effort to suggest the relative importance of the various anomalies. And there have not been many attempts to indicate why the seeming irrationalities in economic behavior take place so frequently in some cases and so much less so in others. Such efforts are essential if we are to have a better notion of where to turn our attention to first. Moreover, there have been few efforts to explain why some deviations from what has been termed rational behavior continue to be little affected while others disappear with repetition.

Experimental economics began in the late 1940s and gained renewed importance by the late 1970s. At first, it was oriented primarily to validating received microeconomic theory. Then it was further stimulated by experimental work in psychology that seemed to cast doubts on the behavioral assumptions of traditional economic theory. This presentation outlines the results of that portion of experimental economics that relates to behavioral economics. Reference also will be made to field (natural) experiments, which may hold even more promise as a means of ascertaining the generality of the behavioral assumptions. Some attention also will be given to speculations about evolutionary factors in explaining human tendencies in decision making that may have taken place over time.

Readers seeking more background are referred to the Second Edition of Edward Cartwright's *Behavioral Economics* (London, 2014; Routledge), to Daniel Kahneman's, *Thinking Fast and Slow* (New York, 2011: Farrar, Straus and Giroux and since, translated into many languages), to Richard Thaler's *Misbehaving. The Making of Behavioral Economics* (New York, 2015; Norton) and to the articles cited in those books. A few additional references are mentioned along the way. Add to this, the concise entries in *Real-World Decision Making. An Encyclopedia of Behavioral Economics*, edited by Morris Altman (Santa Barbara, CA and Denver, Co. 2015: Greenwood).

2

HISTORICAL BACKGROUND

It is almost always possible to dig up historical antecedents, and so it is for behavioral economics. Perhaps what is most relevant is what those who formulated the antecedents finally employed as their *modus operandi*. Adam Smith mentioned a number of important behavioral concepts in a volume published nearly two decades before *The Wealth of Nations* in 1776, most notably, the central proposition of Prospect Theory discussed in Section 6; unfortunately, the key behavioral concepts do not seem to have made it into the subsequent, more celebrated book. Similarly, some of the notions of prominent mid-Nineteenth Century economists would seem to lend themselves to a behavioral approach, but that was not their emphasis. Psychological factors, even the possibility of refutable empirical assumptions, entered into the analysis of several late Nineteenth Century economists, but this was at an early stage of the formal development of psychology when the first experiments focused more on what economics assumed about human behavior. As psychology developed further and the findings of experiments were less along the lines of what our discipline assumed, economic theory abandoned reference to psychology.

Irving Fisher, perhaps the most prominent American economist of the first half of the 20th Century, voiced behavioral concerns, but that is not what emerges most prominently in his writings and it is not what he is known for today. John Maynard Keynes wrote of "animal spirits" and considered several implications of a behavioral nature (in his personal investments as well as in his theorizing), but that is not what the gist of Keynesian economics is about and what almost all of his followers (and those who have taken issue with them) have focused on. To this day, macroeconomics, the branch of economics that deals with the economic consequences of the economy as a whole, has lagged in its incorporation of behavioral economics. (There are several apparent exceptions to this. The work on social norms and happiness dealt with later in this offering, certainly are macro topics. Bewley's interview approach described below, though micro in character, reflects that author's efforts to obtain better bases for macroeconomic analyses. However, he does not deal with the degree to which different deviations from rationality have particular macroeconomic consequences. Some of the most interesting efforts to apply a behavioral approach to macroeconomics can be found in the work of Robert Shiller, summarized in the third edition of *Irrational Exuberance* [Princeton, 2015, Princeton University Press], particularly in the revision of his Nobel Lecture section on the Implications for Financial Innovation.)

Pareto and Walras introduced the concepts—and the mathematical expression of those concepts—that have driven economics since the early 20th Century, particularly since the end of the Second World War. Equilibrium and optimization concepts have dominated, along with national income concepts since the 1930s. Economics has remained essentially a positive discipline, particularly microeconomics, the latter, even more so following mathematician Von Neumann and economist Morgenstern's game theory with its proclamation of the axioms of rational behavior. Recommendations concerning economic behavior and economic policy were always recognized to be more normative, but both were assumed to follow from positive economics. Even so, most of the profession has felt that economic policy goes beyond the increasingly scientific economics, and involves political and philosophical considerations.

There were those who raised particular concerns about the behavioral assumptions of the prevailing economic theory, of course, particularly in the Twentieth Century. Thorstein Veblen spoke of conspicuous consumption and "keeping up with the Joneses" in the 1920s. This was picked up in the 1950s and '60s by others who introduced the relative income hypothesis and stressed positional concerns. A few voiced questions about the efficiency with which resources were combined, but mainly outside Economics Departments—particularly in business schools.

At a more formal level, several economists did make important contributions. Maurice Allais showed that economists' behavioral assumptions of rationality were not always what their choices revealed (not even the choices of professional economists), and Daniel Ellsberg indicated that the *source* of any uncertainty between choices can affect the outcome, contrary to what rational behavior would predict (and that that uncertainty could delay decision making). Allais' important contribution in this field appeared in French, and was largely ignored by English speaking economists for many years. Indeed, it was not even the main thrust of his own work in economics, and was essentially dismissed by leading economists and statisticians. The psychologist Ward Edwards tended to support the notion that people generally behaved essentially in a rational manner, but he indicated that they did not tend to incorporate new information in a strictly rational manner (they acted conservatively, he maintained). He succeeded in getting a brilliant group of psychology students to examine decision making, including several who were to become famous for contributing to behavioral economics. Economists did not read the work of psychologists at that time, however. They considered that behavioral matters were covered by Friedman's optimization and "as if" assumptions about human behavior, and were not really of further interest to economic science. Ellsberg's contribution was assigned more often in theory classes in the 1960s and '70s, but he became remembered most for his association with political matters ("the Ellsberg Papers," which dealt with the war in Vietnam). Thomas Schelling was often cited for his application of game theory to decision making in the Cold War. Harry Markowitz singled out the importance of myopic gains and losses rather than overall wealth in influencing decision making, but he was awarded a Nobel Prize for his more rationalist work in financial analysis and his behavioral work was ignored by most in the economics profession—until later, when it was resurrected by the psychologists Daniel Kahneman and

Amos Tversky (with Markowitz himself then becoming an active advocate of behavioral economics).

The first, major breakthrough regarding behavior came with the work of Herbert Simon and the Carnegie School (the School of Industrial Management, not the Economics Department). Simon, received his Ph.D. in political science, and taught operations research (being a pioneer in artificial intelligence) and psychology as well as economics, obtaining a Nobel Prize in the latter in 1978. One of Simon's first efforts, with Alan Newell, was to develop heuristics for business as a second best alternative to optimizing calculations that were not deemed feasible. Interviews that he, his colleagues and students held with businesspeople led to recognition of widespread slack in the efficiency with which resources were utilized, and to affirmations about the cognitive limitations of humans, along with dissenting hypotheses about their underlying motivations. The concept of Bounded Rationality was formulated to take account of both—though it was later used by traditional economists to suggest constrained maximization in a more traditional sense. Simon, his group and, later, the evolutionary economists, Sidney Winter and Richard Nelson, wrote of Aspirations and Satisficing, and also of *procedural* rationality. The latter was offered as an alternative to the end-tem, substantive rationality emphasized by mainstream economists, and reflected the limitations imposed by the computational ability of humans, the time in which a decision had to be made, imperfect memory, problems of perception, and, importantly, context. This more behavioral view began to gain adherents, especially by those who taught in business schools, but among most economists, the reaction was highly adverse. That may have been in part because of the seeming conflict between aspirations and satisficing, on the one hand, and on procedural rationality, on the other (though some mainstream economists came to take Simon's satisficing to mean an approximation to optimization).

3

METHODOLOGICAL CONSIDERATIONS

Since the time of Adam Smith and especially during the last half of the Twentieth Century, behaviorally oriented economists cited individual exceptions to the notions that economic actors functioned as self-serving maximizers, that enterprises were engaged in maximizing profits, and that prices were uniform in different markets, but these never truly registered among economists for the reasons already mentioned and because of the presumed ability of arbitrage to eliminate economic discrepancies in short order. (However, in the 1980s, Fischer Black, an eminent financial economist, active on Wall Street as well as in the academy, wrote a straightforward and highly convincing piece concerning the limits of arbitrage.) The basic model of economics was held to reflect what happened and to predict well. Moreover, it was also maintained that many deviations from rationality were offset by others, and, in any event, that those deviations were not predictable.

Economists had come to conclude that their theories should be characterized by parsimony, generality, tractability, and as would be added, at least plausibility—the essential congruence of those theories with reality. Attitudes among economists began to change with accumulating evidence from cognitive psychology (notably that branch of cognitive analysis known as behavioral decision theory) and experimental economics.

Experimental economics had begun as a means of testing (and affirming) microeconomic theory, but prodded by what they regarded as disturbing results from experiments by psychologists, initially skeptical experimental economists like David Grether and Charles Plott, came to reveal an increasing number of anomalies in economic behavior.

While such experiments did not prove anything, those conducting them encountered so many deviations from the rationality they had assumed— "anomalies" they termed them—that an increasing number of economists (and especially their graduate students) began to wonder about the universality and usefulness of the rationality assumption of traditional economic models; some economists also began to question what exactly was involved in what they had been referring to as rationality. Even though the laboratory experiments employed many controls not found in the real world (they ignored incentives initially, and they have continued to include a lack of the deception so important in many real world transactions, along with an absence of learning—though traditional game theorists now consider learning, even if only that produced by the experience of highly structured games). Moreover, the participants in experiments were primarily inexperienced first and second year college students, generally in elite colleges. Even so, the often less-than-completely rational findings began to register. Results seeming to cast doubt on the traditional assumption of rational behavior also were found in field (natural) experiments. These results, such as inconsistent responses of physicians to differently framed diagnoses of identical disease situations (described by Daniel Kahneman and Amos Tversky) and the seemingly inconsistent responses of citizens to differently framed auto insurance requirements of two neighboring states in the U.S., provided more serious evidence in favor of a behavioral approach. (Later, studies such as a convincing one by John List of other-than-strictly rational behavior in the market for sports cards were produced.) Together, laboratory and field experiments have constituted the principal empirical evidence of behavioral economics.

Another source of empirical evidence comes from open-ended, in-depth interviews of economic actors, asked to explain how they made particular decisions (and, in a few cases, observed while in the process of making their decisions). That would seem to be consistent with the increasing recognition of emotional factors, even in dominantly cognitive decision making. While some of that work has been praised, most behavioral economists regard this approach for generating hypotheses about decision making behavior as too time consuming and unscientific. (Most behavioral economists appear to be satisfied with the hypotheses revealed in laboratory and field experiments, which, it has been insisted, can easily be duplicated.) Note, though, that List and two other prominent experimenters are now testing some of the behavioral hypotheses uncovered by the most serious of the interview-based studies, that published by Truman Bewley.

Behavioral economics has come to be regarded more seriously by economists as a consequence of the studies of experimental economics and the mathematical formulation given to Prospect Theory, the most prominent of the behavioral theories, which is considered in Section 6.

Open-ended, in-depth interview-based studies appear to have been undertaken only by this author and Truman Bewley to date. The Schwartz studies, admittedly rudimentary, were published in 1987, 1998 2004, 2006, and 2010, with a further effort prepared in 2012. The studies focused on manufacturing industries in the United States and Latin America. Those interview-based efforts point to a number of findings that probably could not have been obtained in laboratory or traditional field experiments, and to others that might be more amenable to resolution by experiments, but for which none appear to have been undertaken.

Truman Bewley, the other author (a mathematician as well as an economist), teaches General Equilibrium Theory at Yale University, continues primarily in that field and does not regard himself as a behavioral economist. Nonetheless, he was disturbed enough by the seeming unrealism of the behavioral assumptions of the models he had to work with, that he took time out to interview more than 300 firms, labor leaders and consultants about wage formation, and is currently completing a study concerning price formation that has involved nearly 600 interviews. The first set of interviews and the resulting study, *Why Wages Don't Fall During a Recession* (Cambridge, MA, 1999; Harvard University Press), were based on findings occurring during the relatively short 1990-1991 recession in the United States. His major conclusion was that morale—which he defined to include both unconsciously and consciously felt mental and physical factors—influences productivity, and, in turn, profitability. His interviews led him to maintain that except for those cases in which there were severe impacts in the financial condition of enterprises that were obvious to employees, or in which there were sharp declines in the economy as a whole, the morale of those employed is affected more by wage reductions than by layoffs.

A few economists had published articles which *assumed* that the morale of those on the job might be adversely affected by wage cuts (most notably, George Akerlof), though without any indication as to whether morale might be affected differently if wages were not reduced but, instead, some workers were laid off. It is difficult to imagine how insights concerning the differential impact on worker morale under those alternative situations could be obtained in highly controlled laboratory experiments with students, particularly if the usually youthful and inexperienced laboratory participants were asked to respond in a manner that assumed that they had been long employed and had become dependent on their wages for the well-being of their families. (Nor have there been experiments in which the participants were workers, also confronted with the two types of situations, and in which the studies were carried out in comparable or even more normal times.) The current efforts of several experimental economists may deal more satisfactorily with Bewley's findings regarding wage cuts and layoffs. Bewley's study also came to several other conclusions that might be more readily verified in the laboratory, but do not seem to have been. He found, for example, that labor unions and employees generally did not seem particularly concerned with severance pay (at least, not during relatively short downturns such as the one he studied), and that informational asymmetries do not seem to explain wage rigidity, despite the importance that the latter have been accorded in some theories of labor economics. The lessons from the two studies were summarized in an article Bewley published in the *Journal of Socio-Economics* in 2002 entitled, "Interviews as a Valid Empirical Tool in Economics."

4

PREFERENCES

Even though critical, traditional economic analysis dispenses quickly with preferences. They are what they are, say some economists, and though they are based on attitudes and values, there is little need to explain them or to deal with any problems they may appear to present. We document them with "indifference curves," but the explanations of why they are as they are is said to belong to psychology and other fields of study. Preferences involve rankings. Though they may change, notably in the long run, they are said to be relatively stable, reflecting what sometimes amounts to a status quo bias.

What can be said, according to traditional economic theory, is that preferences should reflect the principles of rationality. A leading text puts all this together by stating that the preferences of traditional economics should adhere to basic rules of logic and probability theory, that they should be coherent, and that they should not be formed on the basis of immaterial or irrelevant factors. They should simply reflect what's in the best interests of the decision maker. (Nonetheless, an increasing number of more or less traditional economists have begun to write about notions of multiple selves and Meta or basic preferences. Context is now also given more attention, along with matters such as the relative levels of assets.)

Behavioral economics, as a descriptive approach, has introduced a number of qualifications—in addition to increased insistence on context and the relative level of assets. **The first of these qualifications is that preferences should not be entirely incompatible with empirical observations**. This does not mean that assumptions must echo real life (often impossible and too narrow to cover significant categories), but the dictum rules out insisting that something as basic as that the economic theory of descriptive economics should be exempt from observation. Beyond this, behavioral economics has staked out a number of additional explanatory factors concerning the assumptions about human behavior.

Psychologists have shown that differences in framing (differences in the way in which events are described) can lead to short run shifts in preferences, even to what has been termed preference reversal. Different words lead to different descriptions of the same situation, as marketing specialists and trial lawyers have long shown they were well aware. Mortality and survival rates trigger different responses, even when obviuisly referring to the exactly the same results—even among professionals accustomed to dealing with those data. Different words evoke different heuristics or rules of thumb, many of which do not have the same consequences for decision making; the leading explanation for the shift in preferences is that different words tend to produce different emotional reactions and a resort to different heuristics—heuristics characterized as affective, in this case. Cognitive factors sometimes enter as well.

Experiments in this area in the early 1970s by psychologists Paul Slovic and Sarah Lichtenstein led to documentation of preference reversal which so shook up the economics profession that several leading economic experimenters (notably Grether and Plott) attempted to disprove the results—an effort that was not successful by their own accounts. In the initial experiments of the psychologists, participants were asked to choose between (1) a bet with a high probability of winning a small amount of money, and (2) another bet, with a smaller chance of winning a larger amount. The expected values were approximately the same. The participants were then asked to value each bet by stating the minimum amount they would accept to sell each of the bets if they had proprietary rights over them (or the maximum amount they would pay to buy the gamble). Most of those who preferred the first bet assigned a larger value to the second bet, and vice versa for those who had preferred the second bet. The results were subsequently replicated in a Las Vegas casino. The choices based on dollars differed from those based on the indicated preferences and probability. Preference reversal implies intransitivity (preferring A to B and B to C but not A to C), the failure of procedural invariance, or a deficiency in the payoff scheme used to elicit the cash equivalence of preferences. Studies (notably by Slovic, Tversky and Kahneman) show that potentially very disconcerting lack of transitivity is rarely the cause of preference reversal. The most usual explanation is procedural invariance, the words used and the way in which solicitation is sought matters. Leading experimental economists showed subsequently that repetitions of the same type of experiment with participants who are given a chance to observe the results tends to lead to a reduction or an elimination of preference reversal—but, in real life, many decision choices are unique and even similar ones often are spaced too far apart in time to be accurately recalled and thus to reflect greater consistency.

Second, preferences may differ according to a person's endowment—his or her possessions—at least for goods that are not intended for immediate resale. This was shown in a series of experiments in the 1980s by Richard Thaler and several others (see the summaries in Thaler's 2015 book, *Misbehaving*, cited at the end of Section 1). Such a finding goes against the basic notion of traditional economics, that whether someone is a buyer or seller of an item depends solely on its price. Most economists now accept the concept of an endowment effect despite its adverse implications for the discipline's fundamental indifference curve analysis and for the notion of gains from trade. Fortunately, the endowment effect does not appear to hold, or to be very pronounced, for most categories of goods that are ordinarily bought and sold. The initial experiments were made with such articles as drinking mugs containing a university emblem and inexpensive pens, neither of which were intended for resale. While the endowment effect does not appear to hold for most individual goods, it does seem to be important for discerning the different preferences of the rich and those at the other end of the income spectrum. The general level of assets does influence preferences and has been shown to be important in studies of poverty and social classes, especially in developing countries. The endowment effect may also help explain why there is often such a difference between the price of a home, as evaluated by a buyer, and that seen by a seller in addition to ordinary negotiation considerations. Experiments by behavioral economists could help resolve the uncertainties about the importance of endowment.

Third, experiments have shown that the introduction of less preferred and presumably irrelevant options can influence choice. That is not rational, and, in part, may reflect the difficulty humans have in dealing with large numbers of variables at the same time and of perceiving accurately, all of the consequences of the choices. (It may also reflect other factors, considered later.) Experiments by behavioral economists should help pinpoint where differences in the importance of presumably irrelevant factors matter (or matter most), and where context plays a role in their significance.

Fourth, psychologists Kahneman and Tversky have shown that preferences may vary with alternative reference points (specific contexts), even at the same point in time. This is an important consideration, given the significance assigned to reference points in Prospect Theory (see Section 6). Experimental or other analytical work to deal with this is an absolute necessity. (See Kahneman's *Thinking, Fast and Slow* for his discussion of reference points.)

Fifth, preferences on certain matters, particularly those involving one or more options that are unknown, or may not yet have been formulated, may first have to be constructed. Despite the importance of this point, insisted upon by psychologists Tversky and Slovic (see especially Slovic's "The Construction of Preferences"), most behavioral economists have tended to ignore it. Note, though, that it builds on Simon's observation that in real world decision making, one of the key impediments to choice is that some of the options may not be known and search is necessary to determine them. The economist, Plott, arrived at a somewhat similar conclusion, writing of *discovered* hypotheses (and preferences), but most economists seem to ignore the notion that some preferences may have to be constructed. The contexts in which constructed or discovered preferences matter has been too long overlooked and cries out for attention.

Sixth, preferences may shift quite a bit over time. While most economists do not deny the possibility of major shifts in preferences over time, they have nonetheless assumed that such major shifts in preferences do not occur, even over moderate periods of time, amounting to a kind of a status quo bias. To the extent that economists do allow for major shifts in preferences over time, they tend to ascribe it to major changes in context, or, at least, to an anchoring and adjustment response (described more fully later). Additional factors may be involved, however. Experimental work is indicated.

Preferences also may be influenced by what have been termed "menu effects"—general attraction effects—momentum effects, perhaps influenced by social interaction, and by context as well as by what have been termed visceral effects (see Section 11), to mention a few factors. Yet another consideration sometimes affecting preferences is the level of happiness. Many behavioral economists would be hesitant to give much credence to these— though a substantial number of financial analysts take momentum effects seriously and development specialists have noted many differences and shifts in preferences. Many economists would refer to aspiration levels in determining overall preferences, exemplified in a study by several prominent behavioral economists to the effect that the work decisions of taxi cab drivers seem to reflect daily income targets—though in the advanced economy in which this has been ascertained, it has only been ascertained for those just starting out as taxi drivers; unfortunately, the percentage of novices is generally low and the degree to which all taxi drivers have income targets is unclear. The oft-cited momentum effect and the concept of target incomes are often alluded to and need to be grounded on more case studies.

A problem for researchers lies in unraveling preference falsification by those being questioned or surveyed and even by those whose choices are just being viewed. Finally, going beyond those specializing in behavioral decision theory, some psychologists have followed Maslow and maintained that preferences are determined by a hierarchy of needs, beginning with physiological needs, and extending to needs for security, a sense of belonging, self-respect and personal realization. A larger number of psychologists would conclude that preferences are affected by motivations, which have been described as influenced by Need for Achievement, Locus of Control, Sensation Seeking and Risk Taking, Altruism, Time Preference, Life Style, An Inclination for Changes in Preference, and Cognitive Abilities. Very few behavioral economists have dealt with these concepts, though Simon did explain the decision making choices of even some middle level corporate members as involving a form of altruism (See especially, Simon, "A Mechanism for Social Selection and Successful Altruism," *Science*, Vol. 250, pp. 1665-68; and Simon, "Altruism and Economics," *American Economic Review*, Vol. 83, No.2). Nobel laureate Shiller assigns a great deal of importance to motivational factors in financial decision making.

5

HEURISTICS OR RULES OF THUMB

Heuristics or Rules of Thumb are means of reducing the search necessary to find a solution to a problem. They are shortcuts that provide subjectively compelling substitutes for the use of probabilities in making judgments. Heuristics are particularly important in the presence of uncertainty but also where many factors enter into decision making and the pressure of time or the deliberation costs are major considerations. We turn to heuristics especially when engaged in what Kahneman refers to as "thinking fast,' but, often, also when "thinking slowly" and relying more on cognitive processes.

Some of the first academic heuristics were aimed at approximating optimization but with the work of the behavioral decision theorists, more heuristic models have sought to capture the way in which real-world choices were made, sometimes involving what has been referred to as mental models—and that does not always involve doing what's in the best interests for an organization or an individual. The initial efforts have been referred to as the heuristics and biases program, with the deviations from what traditional economics would regard as rational calculation characterized as biases. Principal focus has been on the general heuristics outlined by Kahneman and Tversky, especially since their short but highly influential article in *Science* in the mid-1970s. Although the program began with an emphasis on cognitive processes, Kahneman acknowledges that emotional or affective factors always were deemed to be present. An objective of the heuristics and biases program has been to categorize the deviations from what is indicated as optimal by rational choice models, and to improve heuristics so as to reduce those biases or to take them into account in decision making. It has been shown that contrary to the expectations of leading mainstream economists, most deviations from optimality are not random but often systematic and predictable. Unfortunately, there is no accepted theory of heuristics and the use of different heuristics can lead to different results. Gird Gigerenzer and associates focus more on the development of specific heuristics (see, e. g., Gerd Gigerenzer, Peter Todd and the ABC Research Group, *Simple Heuristics That Make Us Smart*), and given the limitations imposed by human abilities and time constraints, they have been critical of a biases approach, focusing instead on the relative accuracy of "fast and frugal" heuristics compared to the results of more comprehensive calculation. They regard their work as following in the tradition of Simon's procedural rationality. (See especially, Simon, "From Substantive to Procedural Rationality," in S. J. Latsis, ed., *Method and Appraisal in Economics*, pp. 129-148; and "Rationality as a Process and as a Product of Thought," *American Economic Review*, Vol. 68, No. 2, pp. 1-16.)

There are a number of reasons for using heuristics:

- Decision makers may be unaware of an available, optimal way to solve a problem, and may not have the resources or access to credit to obtain help—or the deliberation costs involved may be greater than the added benefits of the "optimal" solution.
- Decision makers may be unable to obtain all the information necessary for an optimizing solution, or may not be able to do so by the time a decision must be made. Even if they can obtain all the information, they may not be able to complete the optimizing calculations in time.
- While optimization techniques may be feasible, they may not yet have been devised for some types of problems.
- Where there are multiple objectives, unique, optimal solutions are unlikely.

- The use of heuristics that can be applied rapidly may enable decision makers to keep certain matters secret until they decide to make the decision known. (This may be important where several alternatives to decision making are available.)
- The problem may not be in obtaining information, but in perceiving it correctly and avoiding attempts to deal with what is actually a variant of the true problem.
- An extraordinary amount of information may overwhelm decision makers, and this may be magnified by the emotional character of the decision, the state of the decision maker at the time, and/or by stress and what some neurologists have characterized as decision fatigue, following a series of difficult decisions in a relatively short period of time.
- Seemingly winning formulas of some market participants over considerable periods of time, but involving increased risk and uncertainty may lead astray some of those who would ordinarily avoid such approaches.
- The use of heuristics may be called for if implementation of what is optimally calculated presents major problems.
- The use of heuristics and reliance on intuition may be the only plausible approach in cases of appreciable uncertainty.

The use of heuristic shortcuts is most appropriate where they closely approximate the result of optimization calculations. "Fast and frugal" heuristics are called for in situations in which there are "flat maxima" in which several options lead to similarly high rates of return.

As Simon (and subsequently Nelson and Winters) indicated, mainstream economics provides a suitable set of tools for dealing with a well-defined, clearly enunciated and usually small set of alternatives. Unfortunately, decision makers frequently confront a poorly defined set of choices and often confront many alternatives. Moreover, the first major challenge may arise in the search for the more important options and in recognition of the consequences of those options. Indeed, in many cases the decision maker may even have to construct preferences in order to be able to proceed intelligently. For decisions based on evolving technologies, some private decision makers have observed that heuristics which aid in horizon scanning are often more useful than those that emphasize care in final calculations. This is not to deny that decision makers sometimes fail to take advantage of available optimization mechanisms when they are appropriate, or that they use incorrect heuristics or fail to take biases into account.

There should be guidelines for the formation (and improvement) of heuristics, the search for information with given heuristics (including "stopping rules" as stressed by the Gigerenzer Group), and for the way in which a decision should be made using the information obtained.

5.1 The Categories of Heuristics and Their Biases

Tversky and Kahneman considered three general purpose heuristics: representativeness, availability, and anchoring and adjustment. The psychologist Slovic later brought together the work of a number of researchers on the role of emotional considerations which he characterized as the Affect Heuristic. Others wrote of several additional categories of general purpose heuristics.

Heuristics usually have been referred to as shortcuts to solutions which involve biases, the latter sometimes quite large. As noted, an exception to this approach has come from the work of Gigerenzer and the Max Planck Institute. Gigerenzer, Selten and colleagues hark back to Simon and the focus on procedural rationality. Their approach emphasizes specific heuristics. For them, the emphasis on biases is misplaced, and indeed, they show that the heuristics they develop—often termed fast and frugal heuristics—sometimes perform as well (or nearly as well) as the results of full calculation. They stress that the heuristics are shaped by the environment and the prevailing context. It has been claimed, however, that the fast and frugal approach is subject to the bias of selecting overly familiar factors, and, at any rate, does not perform well in making judgments unless the rate of return is roughly comparable for alternative options.

Problems may arise in acquiring information including considerations related to availability, perception, the frequency (and order) of data presentation, and the concreteness and vividness of information. Availability biases may arise as a result of the ease with which people can recall specifics from memory (at least in certain contexts). The content of specifics also may influence assessments about their relative importance. Availability acquisition biases can lead to overestimation of the probability of well-publicized, dramatic or recent events, leading to what have been termed availability cascades. A prominent example is the belief that most people have is that homicides are more common than suicides, though the reverse has been well documented. Imperfect perception also can be serious and is often accentuated by differences in education, life experiences, personality, and context including societal differences.

Biases in processing information may begin with an incorrect understanding of information. There is a tendency to give undue weight to certainty, even the appearance of certainty, particularly in cases involving several steps in which there is certainty only in a final step. Low probabilities present particular difficulties, often being overestimated, but are sometimes underestimated and occasionally ignored. True probabilities are not recognized on occasion because of the use of data from too short a time period (recall the 1990s calculations of the mathematicians and Nobel laureates of Long Term Capital Management) and also because of failure to understand interconnections and overall economic or macroeconomic effects.

Errors that arise in evaluating statistical relationships can lead to the selection of inappropriate heuristics. There are illusory associations, a tendency to automatically attribute causality to correlation, inappropriate use of linear extrapolations, and incorrect approaches to estimating nonlinear extrapolations. Failure to incorporate new information correctly or even consistently is common. Moreover, we often seek results that confirm our anticipations, prejudices, and past results rather than seek contrary evidence as we should. And we tend to ignore the fact that models based on the enunciated criteria of experts have been shown to be better predictors than the ongoing judgments of those same experts.

The heuristic, representativeness, involves judgments of the likelihood of an event or identification, based on its similarity to a class of events or individuals—based on its seeming fit. There are no uniform guidelines on the degree to which representativeness affects judgments of likelihood. Use of the heuristic sometimes reflects a failure to take account of available data on the statistical incidence of those belonging to particular groups (base-rate information) and, beyond that, of the so-called "law of small numbers." Early experiments by psychologists showed that experiment participants tended to ignore even available base-rate data and focus on stereotyped personality characteristics in judging professional occupations. Characteristics often identified with certain groups of individuals were given more weight in identifying the group to which particular individuals belonged than base rate data—which often implied that the individuals in question are unlikely to belong to those groups. Representativeness considerations appear to underlie much human reasoning by analogy.

Failure to allow for "regression toward the mean," a bias associated with representativeness, is perhaps best exemplified by the so-called "hot hand" in basketball and other sports in which most individuals tend to expect good results to be repeated without taking adequate account of the less satisfactory ones that also are a part of what has been experienced. Another major bias is the conjunction bias, in which someone or something is irrationally judged to be more probable than the larger group to which the person or matter obviously belongs. A prominent example is found in the Kahneman-Tversky example in which participants identified Linda as a feminist bank teller even more often than as a bank teller.

Availability is the heuristic reflecting the weight given to information in place of probability, basically because of the ease of recall. That ease of recall may be due to some recent dramatic event. Unfortunately, there is no agreement as to what constitutes a different degree of availability or the weight that should be given to differences in availability. The main bias of the availability heuristic is due to its extreme lack of sensitivity to sample size.

Anchoring and adjustment is a heuristic that involves adjustment from some starting point. The latter may refer to recent data such as the current rate of inflation or economic growth. Often, the factors explaining the starting point are less known or understood by those making the judgments. The anchor may involve random and even false data injected by individuals serving as "plants" hired by the organizers of experiments, who are instructed to respond with irrelevant data, sometimes those that just happen to be known to experiment participants such as the last four digits of their social security number.

Heuristics, particularly the representative heuristic, may lead to overconfidence. Indeed, overconfidence seems to be a general characteristic of human response, presenting itself even in assumptions about data such as the basic facts that constitute elements of a decision problem. Experiments have shown that even when people are asked only to indicate information of which they are absolutely certain, they often respond including information of which they are less than fully certain. Yet excess confidence makes people feel good and moves them to do things that they might not otherwise have done, and this appears to be an important explanation of much entrepreneurial activity. Overconfidence is sometimes attributable to an illusion of control and to an exaggeration of what can be expected even from better-than-average capability. Overconfidence seems to be a common phenomenon (which is not to deny the defective nature of some alleged proofs of overconfidence). Evidence suggests that most people believe they are better-than-average drivers or citizens and that their children are better than average (at least in many respects). Yet some individuals express less confidence than warranted, particularly in certain contexts. Both extremes can bias results.

Problems with memory, discussed below in Section 10, also introduce biases into heuristics. Another common factor, particularly of the representative heuristic, is a status quo bias, which characterizes much reasoning that does not involve complete calculation and also may involve substantial uncertainty.

Several other general heuristics have been receiving more attention recently, notably the automated choice heuristic, choosing by default (becoming more common in savings and investment decisions), regret theory (which often leads to results similar to prospect theory but for which there is mixed empirical support), and especially, loss aversion, first observed as a particularly frequent anomaly in revealing seemingly altered attitudes toward risk. Regret theory refers to decisions undertaken to avoid possible outcomes that would be regarded as particularly disappointing and thus regretted; it features a bias towards conventional choice. Loss aversion refers to tendency of individuals to value negative outcomes more than expected values that reflect the actual probabilities of those outcomes. While there may not have been enough effort to document loss aversion, it's clear that there is a tendency towards the phenomenon. Unfortunately, that tendency seems to vary quite a bit and, indeed, there are situations in which there does not seem to be any loss aversion at all. In any event, note that both regret theory and loss aversion are not just cognitive heuristics; they usually involve strong affective components as well.

For many problems, a solution requires more than a single heuristic. Such heuristics may take into account the type of decision making involved, the particular context, and the likely importance of missing information. To do this, data on heuristics and their biases should be recorded to be sure that they are adequately taken into account, and so that there will be a solid basis for improving the heuristics. Unfortunately, even decision makers who systematically record numerous data points, rarely make written note of the considerations underlying the heuristics and biases that are often the most important determinants in making a decision.

There are only a few published guidelines for determining the size and significance of biases, and for dealing with the predictive use of heuristics. In addition, some problems are so complex that they cannot be solved in a reasonably efficient manner in the time available. Such problems may lend themselves to solution by an even less formal and structured approach--by pure intuition or by a kind of expertise that has been referred to as pattern recognition. (This is more complex than what is described as the use of recognition heuristics by the Gigerenzer Group.) Pattern recognition seems to be the secret of success of Grand Masters in chess, and, it would seem, that of the Warren Buffets in the worlds of business and investment.

A major issue in processing information is how people frame information, which is dealt with in more detail in Section 6. Dubious recall of data, imperfect perception of data, and imperfect feedback can impede decision making. The presence of many options, some irrelevant, can distort judgment, apparently more with some heuristics than others. Context, the available modes of communication, and even the physical and emotional state of a decision maker can influence the heuristic chosen. Hindsight bias also can be an obstacle, as certainly, the misunderstanding of chance fluctuations and the nature of statistics generally, does. The most common biases affecting heuristics are attributable to loss aversion, lack of sufficient sensitivity to sample size, failure to allow for regression to the mean, conjunction situations of the type described above, overconfidence, undue anchoring, inappropriate framing of information, and inattention to probabilities.

5.2 The Affect Heuristic

An affect heuristic provides a first and almost automatic reaction to stimuli, often with little or no conscious reasoning. It tends to orient information processing and judgment. An affect heuristic generally involves what psychologists term the experiential system, drawing on past experiences, particularly those of given societies. It incorporates images marked by positive or negative feelings that provide clues for judgment and decision making. Such imagery has been shown to influence people's preferences for visiting specific cities, their reaction to certain technologies, their views favoring health-enhancing behavior such as stopping smoking or eating healthier foods, in their inclinations to invest in new versus old companies and in "growth" stocks, and in a wide variety of decisions in less developed, more traditional communities. The stronger the emotional element, the greater the tendency to ignore probability. (Along similar lines, but perhaps even more difficult to explain in rational terms, note that a four-fifths finding usually carries more weight than an identical probability finding of .8, and often, even more weight than actual numbers. Often, but, alas, not always—which points to one of the serious difficulties of resorting to a behavioral approach, and of employing the same models for all cases.) Judgments are influenced by the precision of affective impressions. Another consideration is that most respondents react more favorably to the likelihood of winning (a lottery for example) than to the actual monetary payoff (at least for lotteries other than those with very large payoffs, though, unfortunately, the dividing line between lotteries in general and very large lotteries is not clear).

The perception of risk is strongly linked to the degree to which a hazard evokes feelings of dread. Affect-laden images of frequencies and individual cases tend to weigh more heavily than probabilities. Somewhat counter to what might seem to be common sense, there is often a negative correlation between judgments about risks and high benefits (seeming to contradict traditional economists' adage that there is no such thing as a free lunch). People assess the perception of the risk of death to be much greater for those adversities heavily reported in the media such as accidents, homicides, fires and tornados than for less publicized causes such as diabetes, asthma, tuberculosis, stroke, heart attacks and even many forms of cancer which carry comparable levels of adversity. Attitudes, moods and context often play a more important role than economic indicators in explaining some jury awards and also the willingness to pay for public goods. Most disturbing, and limiting for the application of a behavioral approach, is the degree to which the empirical findings are qualified by the word "often."

Affective reactions may trigger cognitive reasoning but they also may undermine it, of course. The smiling faces in advertisements for mediocre products can manipulate perceptions of value. Background music can increase interest in very ordinary motion pictures and the favorable comments of well-known personalities, even in the absence of indications of their reasons, can influence the decisions of others. Affective reactions can latterly numb reasoning in some cases, as in smoking (recall the former case of "The Marlboro Man"); similarly, with the current photos of severely diseased persons on cigarette packs (in some countries). A happy mood often increases the likelihood of heuristic processing while a sad mood increases the likelihood of more systematic processing. Affective reactions include those which are visceral such as hunger, tiredness, and fear, most of which are general, along with those that are more strictly emotional and often directed at specific persons or groups.

With all heuristics, much remains to be done to indicate the degree to which their use leads to results which deviate from optimality (to some standard of optimality), and the degree to which results are biased still further by the general failure to record the precise heuristics employed and the biases encountered. For further discussion of the factors underlying the affect heuristics, see Section 11.

6

PROSPECT THEORY AND FRAMING

Use of Prospect Theory (PT) has been the major approach to date for incorporating behavioral factors into economic models. The principal points of Prospect Theory are the following (see also Chapter 26 in the Kahneman volume cited above):

1. Actual decision making responds to *changes* in wealth rather than to *states* of wealth, as traditional economic presentations tend to assume—that is to say, actual decision making usually responds to gains and losses. Initially (in 1979), PT was elaborated with respect to the gains or losses experienced in a single, unspecified reference point (context) though this has been expanded since. It remains for behavioral economists to explain the likelihood of particular reference points and their significance for alternative choices, along with the frequency with which choices are based on changes in wealth rather than states of wealth and the varying degree to which the former occurs.

2. Differences in the attitudes toward risk (differences in risk preferences) can occur even at essentially the same point in time, depending particularly on whether losses are involved. Complexity, the nature of

social interaction and the degree of stress certainly are factors as well. Here, too, work is required to identify the contexts in which there is loss aversion and differences in the significance of such loss aversion.

3. There is a diminishing sensitivity to gains and losses. The precise extent of the diminishing sensitivity needs to be estimated for different contexts.

4. Decision makers do not make choices based strictly on probabilities, but on what they view as prospects, which can be seen as a transformation of those probabilities—by means of heuristics in effect (although K & T did not use that term in their initial article on Prospect Theory). Prospects differ most from probabilities in the case of low probabilities (which are usually overvalued, but sometimes undervalued or ignored). The way in which the objective probabilities are transformed is a major consideration and needs to be indicated.

5. Implicit in PT but not particularly dealt with until after the initial exposition of the theory: the importance of framing, the way in which elements involved in decision making are presented. Also, the matter of narrow vs broad choice (the former representing what has been termed myopic decision making but which may be much more indicated in some cases than in others). While there is no question as to the importance of framing, the significance if its impact varies and needs to be estimated for alternatives if Prospect Theory is to be more useful.

Mainstream economists have been reticent to use Prospect Theory primarily because of the imprecision in the way in which probabilities are said to be modified, and because of the lack of specification regarding reference points.

7

OTHER THEORIES ALTERNATIVE TO EXPECTED UTILITY THEORY

The key consideration to bear in mind is that Prospect Theory is only one way—though it has been the most successful approach to date—of incorporating behavioral factors into economic models. Another approach is the use of regret theory, in which choices are made with consideration of an option that could have been made but was not, but models emphasizing regret are not always well specified and, in any event, have not led to results very different than those of prospect theory. It might be added that affective factors are likely to be even more important than cognitive ones in considering regret theory.

8

MENTAL ACCOUNTS

The key consideration to bear in mind is that economic agents often compartmentalize decisions, whether out of self-control or custom, acting, for example, as if money were not fungible and individual accounts should be evaluated separately, or as if the identifiable components should be evaluated separately rather than together, as part of the larger group or entire sequence to which they belong. That is not to deny that sometimes there may be fewer options than at others to consider the overall effects. One of the principal contributions of mathematics has been to show how much more complicated—and indeterminate—the analysis of mental accounts becomes when one shifts from two to many alternatives. Thaler provides guidelines for selecting one alternative over another when only two options are available, but those guidelines are not adequate when more than two options are presented. In any event, and as another example of how mental accounts enter into decision making, Thaler and his collaborators have shown that the behavior of humans differs when dealing with gambling gains (house money) or other clearly unearned gains than when dealing with gains than strict rationality would allow for. Dealing with "house money" leads to a much greater inclination to take on risks, but that inclination may vary according to the context.

9

INTER-TEMPORAL DISCOUNTING

Most presentations in economics employ the Exponential Discounted Utility Model developed by Paul Samuelson and Tjalling Koopmans to deal with future costs and benefits. In fact, both Samuelson and Koopmans mentioned several concerns with the formulation but they regarded it as a useful standard.

Basically, the traditional approach to discounting in economic analyses assumes a rate of discount that is the same for all periods, for all goods and services, for all quantities, and for all contexts. As a first approximation, income in the future certainly is worth less than present income, not only because investments may fail in absolute terms, but also because one has the option to save and to invest for another day, and to select certain investments over others. Most of us would regard a higher level of income as preferable at certain later times in our lives than others, however, and that begins to cloud matters; similarly, there are times when we know that higher costs in the future are not as bothersome as at certain times in the past. It seems like an unacceptable assumption that every period should be regarded equally if we know that that will not always be the case at the time that decisions are made. Indeed, the assumption that we weigh each time period equally is so counter to actual human judgment that there is a serious question as to whether it should be used, particularly in emphasizing the behavior that is revealed in the real world. Yet that is what is done in traditional economic and business analysis.

Most teachers approve of receiving income each month, in twelve installments rather than earlier, in nine installments, even if they teach for only nine months and have vacation for the remainder of the year. That is to say, they do not object to (and, in fact, most actually prefer) being paid a negative rate of interest. Moreover, most of us prefer to experience increasing levels of income over time rather than the larger sum that might result from receiving a sizable remuneration in the first years (some of which might be invested) and the same or even smaller annual amounts of income thereafter. If the latter were to lead to a higher level of income over the entire period then preference for the rising income profile would not be rational in traditional economic terms, though there might be psychological reasons for preferring it. Many such preferences would seem to be quite predictable. Moreover, while we have long recognized the irrationality of Christmas Club saving accounts, once popular, that pay no interest at all, many of us continue with health club memberships of a financially dubious nature, and in many countries, the highways abound with advertisements for "payday loans" and auto title loans that have interest rates higher than those available to many borrowers. Several affect heuristics play as great a role as the limited opportunities of borrowers. Finally, particularly when it comes to long-term decisions, we sometimes delegate a good deal of our decision choices to others without even knowing the inter-temporal impact of the way in which those experts make their decisions.

These are all behavioral and seemingly irrational human inclinations that were recognized long before the current interest in behavioral economics.

There are a slew of experiments that point to still other "anomalies." The interest rate many demand to make a future level of money seem equivalent to the same level of money at present often varies according to the amount of money involved; 10% more might be required for $100, but for many people who would demand a 10% return for a small amount, 5% would be a high enough if the amount in question were $10,000. Many of us prefer to incur losses immediately rather than later on, and there is a difference in the time required for most of us to regard delays in losses as equivalent to gains in speed-ups. And, as first contended by Adam Smith as far back as 1759 with publication of *The Theory of Moral Sentiments* (and as the prospect theory literature has implied more convincingly), for most people, a given amount of loss is regarded as more significant than the same amount of gains. This holds even more strongly over time for many people.

Many of us would often opt for an ability to reallocate consumption over time—if only we could. In any event, we do not always calculate discount rates according to the utility we gain or lose, as it might seem that we should. Moreover, it is not always clear whether we should be considering the utility we experienced (as best we can recall it), the utility we anticipate (as best we can gauge what it will be), or what some economists have referred to as the relevant rank utility. Inflation and our expectation of inflation, complicates matters, as does uncertainty and ambiguity (the latter of which may even delay making a decision in the first place), and all are likely to differ from time to time. Various visceral influences (more fully explained in Section 11) sometimes enter, as do impulsiveness, temptation, and other emotional factors including the force of self-control, although by varying amounts. They, too, may vary over time. With respect to self-control, consider the matter of procrastination, about which a few words are added below (though one might also want to read David Levine's take on this in *Is Behavioral Economics Doomed?*). Complicating matters still further, experiments reveal different discount rates for costs than for benefits, and, often, for different goods and services, again with the differences frequently changing over time. Worse still, the latter can change in different contexts. Much of this often varies for those of different levels of intelligence, education, experience, and for different cultures, social classes and kinds of upbringing—with the former certainly likely to vary over time.

One response to the above (that many behavioral economists have adopted) is to use hyperbolic rates of discount to reflect the fact that, in general, people tend to be more impatient in the short run, using higher discount rates, and less so in the long run, using lower discount rate—that they have a present bias. That would explain an initial preference for one option and a subsequent shift to another—a shift from a larger benefit later to a smaller one sooner (all the more-so if the latter alternative can be seen or smelled at the time that second decision is made). We later come to regret many of these decisions—but not all, as Robert Frank has shown. (Some such preferences that do not reflect doing the best that is possible are quite deliberate, following from the fact that we sometimes make decisions that take the interests of others into account, even those with whom we are in disagreement and contention.) Hyperbolic rates of discount, along with quasi-hyperbolic rates (a construct in which the impatience is assumed to occur only initially, with the rates of discount the same for each period after that) seem to be replicated much more in everyday decision-making than the discount rates of traditional exponential analysis ordinarily used in economic calculations. They have been used to explain self-regulation, information acquisition, job search, retirement choices, procrastination, addiction, and investment in human capital. The research on hyperbolic discounting suggests that changes in financial markets influence welfare by altering the liquidity of assets, and, as a result, the propensity to consume.

Hyperbolic models do not explain all human behavior better, however, as, e. g., they do not explain the decision of school teachers to accept payment in twelve months for work done in nine, or the general preference for an increasing income profile. Moreover, like the exponential discounting models they replace, most hyperbolic models also tend to assume that economic agents attempt and are able to maximize a utility function, thus ignoring much of the contribution of behavioral decision theory. A major problem with hyperbolic and quasi-hyperbolic models is the lack of an adequate psychological foundation—either a theoretical one or one reflecting the result of empirical work in the field or in laboratories. Where it does prove useful, it is possible that a hyperbolic approach may reflect the way in which humans have evolved in assessing time over centuries, even thousands of years. Moreover, since we now know that costs and benefits reflect the activity of different parts of the brain, it is also quite likely that some of inter-temporal decisions are formulated in one part of the brain, and others, in another part of the brain—which may explain the occasional use of different rates of discount for costs and benefits. But consider, too, that the brain changes over time and may be pushed by contextual or personal factors to change even further.

It is possible to set forth equations for exponential and hyperbolic discounting and to show that the former are better at explaining many inter-temporal decisions and most economics texts do that. Nonetheless, while loss aversion is a general phenomenon, and, so, perhaps to a somewhat lesser extent is prospect theory in general, behavioral economics cannot yet point to a single approach to resolving inter-temporal decisions that copes well with all situations. There are too many situations for which even hyperbolic and quasi-hyperbolic discounting are inadequate. Analysis of individual cases of inter-temporal decision making and subsequent testing of the hypotheses that those cases seem to imply is required. Otherwise we may just be substituting one sometimes inadequate measure for inter-temporal decision making with another. We are not really describing human judgment as behavioral economics sets out to do.

How much we learn from experience seems to vary (consider the persistence of some money illusion over the centuries despite many cautions and some changes in the laws) but there are a number of policy implications. The first defense against generally irrational myopic decisions is to resort to commitment devices—alarm clocks, whole life insurance, illiquid savings accounts, debit cards instead of credit cards, and abstinence. We might even want to consider acting along the lines of Ulysses in the Odyssey (in which, as Robert Strotz recalled in the 1950s, Ulysses had himself tied to the mast and had wax placed in his ears so as to avoid what he knew was the temptation of the sirens). Secondly, greater attention can be given to the cost of switching choices. Finally, more responsibility can be given to government—and private sector entities)—to provide more consumer information, to establish safety requirements, to provide incentives for saving, especially for retirement, to foster environmental safeguards, to add to and maintain infrastructure and social safety nets and to deal with factors such as climate change. (Note, however, the striking differences between the policy recommendations of Great Britain's Stern report on climate change with its low rate of discount and those of the analysis by William Nordhaus, which used presumably more appropriate, higher rates of discount). More comprehensively, there is the Nudge approach, advocated by economist Thaler and lawyer Sunstein, and the still broader approach suggested by several economists at the Kennedy School (see Section 16).

Finally, a word more on procrastination. Procrastination is a common human tendency and is sometimes defended as quite rational but there have been few efforts to explain actual cases of real world procrastination. Academics have come forth with a number of theoretical explanations, however. The most important has been that of Ted O'Donoghue and Mathew Rabin. Procrastination concerns human behavior over time and is characterized in that negative manner because it is a choice that is usually regretted. In the model of O'Donoghue and Rabin, people underestimate the magnitude of the self-control problems and changes in preference. The question is not so much the way in which future benefits are discounted. Rather, the authors state that people tend to put aside an option that involves small benefits and sizable costs in the current period, perhaps often acting myopically. Later (and, indeed, often more than once), they make the same decision again, perhaps reflecting difficulties in self-control when there is no firm commitment. In addition, there also may be a shift in preferences. The latter may be attributable to decision maker recognition of other options or to changes in the environment. The article explains many types of procrastination but might it have been even more revealing if questions had been asked of some of those who procrastinated? In any event, consider also the time factor in the case of drug addiction in which it has been shown that the addiction alters the brain sufficiently to change the way in which the cost-benefit calculation is made.

10

EXPERIENCED UTILITY, MEMORY, AND ANTICIPATED UTILITY

Almost all references by economists to the utility of a project seem to assume that the utility in question is that of the future. Few discuss issues of experienced utility, memory and anticipated utility though this may have begun to change now that psychologists have begun to demonstrate the importance of these matters. Kahneman has been a leading contributor.

Decision making ought to be based on expectations, the utility that is anticipated, of course, since sunk costs and the utility of past occurrences are not all that relevant. Nonetheless, economists' discussion of anticipated utility usually is very much influenced by what was experienced in the past, which, in turn, comes down to the memories of that past. Yet, even to the degree that the future is influenced by some of the same tendencies as those of the past, what we remember may differ from what we actually experienced. Our emotions as well as our general mood tend to influence what we recall of those experiences, along with the context in which we find ourselves. Moreover, our recall is strongly influenced by our reactions at the outset, the end, or certain other moments of that experience, as Kahneman has shown with recollections of the pain associated with certain medical procedures. Rarely do our memories reflect an evenly weighted average of what we recall. We may tend to overestimate probabilities, as the Germans, urged to recall the extraordinarily damaging experience of their country in the early 1920s, overestimate the likelihood (and costs) of inflation more than those in many other countries. Or we may underesti-mate probabilities, along the lines of those who continue to build homes in environmentally vulnerable areas and then, in some cases, even avoid the purchase of subsidized flood insurance (despite a good deal of experience that should lead them to act otherwise).

Finally, consider also what economists have had to say in the past about expectations and how little it has rested on the findings of the other social sciences.

11

VISCERAL AND EMOTIONAL CONSIDERATIONS (AND THE INFLUENCING ROLE OF COMPLETELY IRRELEVANT FACTORS)

It might not seem like it from the traditional exposition of economists, and even from some the initial work in behavioral economics, but human decision making is strongly determined by more than just cognitive factors. Enter, again, Affect Heuristics.

To begin with what might seem to be the most striking consideration, experiments have shown that it is possible to influence choice by introducing factors that are completely irrelevant—factors that are not even as high in preference as others that are not among the most preferred. In addition to the fact that the irrelevant factors may raise emotional reactions, their inclusion also may reflect the fact that choice becomes distorted, with action even paralyzed at times by the presence of a very large number of alternatives, as in the case of considering rational choice in the presence of several dozen breakfast cereals at a typical supermarket. Kahneman notes that adding irrelevant but vivid details to a monetary outcome disrupts calculation. It may be that including irrelevant factors, and especially a large number of factors (even if some are relevant), tends to lead to serious miscalculations of likelihood and to excessively difficult measurements of utility, both of which reinforce the tendency to resort to heuristics that include significant elements of visceral and emotional factors.

We are often taught to think of emotional factors as interfering with rational, cognitive choice, but even before dealing with that, consider an aspect of affective heuristics emanating from what have been termed visceral factors (nicely expounded by the economist/psychologist George Loewenstein). Hunger, thirst, sexual desire, drowsiness, cravings, severe pain, etc., lead to choices of an impulsive nature, with little or no deliberation. They differ from what have usually been characterized as emotions in that they may not be triggered even in part by beliefs, and they are generally not directed against particular individuals or groups (though this is less true of visceral factors such as fear). A deficiency in visceral factors is of consequence in that it may decrease an individual's quality of life, chances of survival, or likelihood of reproducing; a number of these responses seem to have an evolutionary explanation. The need to take visceral factors into account would seem to be stronger for routine than more complex decision making. More often than not, where visceral factors enter into decision making there is an ex post recognition that a better decision would have been made (more rational in traditional economic terms), were it not for the presence of those factors. It tends to be recognized that what was done because of the visceral factors often was not in the best long term interest. Most people do not fully appreciate the influence of visceral factors on current or future behavior, and when asked how a decision was made, they sometimes respond that they came to the decision "by the seat of my pants"—in part to avoid what might be regarded as difficult introspective analysis.

Visceral factors change more rapidly than tastes, are often correlated with certain circumstances and thus are usually predictable, particularly because they tend to take place with little or no conscious cognitive input. Cognitive deliberation, often viewed as a source of stability, can be a source of instability. Visceral factors can produce a split between what one is driven to do and what one regards as best to do, reflecting largely cognitive forces. The decision of alcoholics to take another drink may be an example of this, along with the decision to continue with drugs (although in these cases, in particular, cognitive factors also may be involved). Often people cannot recall exactly what visceral states felt like in the past, which leads them to misjudge their impact in the future; when people are affected strongly by visceral factors—and are acting impulsively—they find it difficult to judge how long it will take for that state to dissipate, and exactly what it will be like when things are more normal and they act more rationally.

Strong visceral factors can influence people's immediate behavior more than they think is justified in normative terms, either beforehand or after those factors have dissipated, and because visceral factors are transient, and generally not accurately recorded, people may underestimate their impact on behavior. This is despite the sometimes important and long-lasting consequences that those factors have for themselves and for society.

Several categories of viscerally affected behavior are of special interest to economics; bargaining behavior, inter temporal choice, motivation and the exertion of effort, self-control and much decision making under risk and uncertainty. Visceral as well as traditional emotional factors may help explain much of the troubling decisions to gamble and yet, at the same time, to purchase insurance (for which many of the efforts of economists to explain miss the boat because they deal solely in cognitive terms), to differ according to gender or age difference, and to engage in sexually risky behavior. People employ a variety of strategies in an effort to limit their own visceral tendencies and those of others, beginning with the use of self-control mechanisms. (Governmental and other societal entities also may play a role.) Taking visceral factors into account seems to help explain some behavior that most people view as simply irrational, and to show that even if it does not conform to cognitive standards of rationality, that it is quite predictable.

What is unclear—and has not been investigated much to date—is the degree to which visceral effects can be offset by incentives (financial and other)—although there is interesting anecdotal evidence that there are at least some individual cases where this takes place. (Consider, for example, the cases of the inventors who persevere despite hunger, lack of sleep and many previous rejections—and consider, more commonly, the case of much human behavior in low income countries and among low income individuals in more advanced economies.) Suffice it to say, economists (even many behavioral economists) have largely ignored visceral factors.

What traditionally have been regarded as emotional factors weigh heavily in decision making, and can be important in triggering decisions to use cognitive calculation as well as in the more commonly cited inclinations to counter cognitive reasoning. Note, too, that although Prospect Theory was dealt with initially as part of cognitive decision theory, emotional factors have been acknowledged to have been important in its formulation, as in the intuitions and other emotional factors that lead to subjective estimations of likelihood weights that differ from those indicated by probability analysis—and in the choice of heuristics to aid in that different valuation. (Kahneman concedes that Tversky and he recognized that even though they were not specific about it when they wrote their seminal *Econometrica* article in 1979.) Visceral and emotional factors, brought together by psychologists as Affect Theory, have been subject to numerous experiments, particularly in developing countries. In addition, social psychology has influenced decision making in several ways, notably with concepts such as Herding, and Groupthink (in which normally rational people become caught up in some Zeitgeist, such as "This time it's different."). Mood swings, the Momentum reaction often associated with Stock Markets, and confidence factors, are also dealt with in the discussion of heuristics and Prospect Theory.

Emotions often involve some cognitive considerations as well as well as physiological arousal and are usually directed towards specific individuals, groups or institutions. Consider anger, hatred, guilt, pride, joy, anxiety, stress, grief, remorse, surprise, boredom, admiration, love, hope and frustration, but also states such as regret. Some emotions are universal, while others seem to be specific to certain cultures. (See the experiments in very different societies grouped together in the publications of Herbert Gintis and Joseph Henrich et al.) There is disagreement concerning the degree to which many emotions can be induced, the role of anticipation emotions, and the extent to which emotions can be controlled—such as the effectiveness of strategies to avoid intensely negative and often counterproductive emotions.

Some illustrations of efforts to induce visceral and more traditional emotional reactions can be seen in advertisements for food products as "natural," cigarettes ads which use that tactic as well as others to minimize the serious risks involved in smoking, ads with smiling faces, and the often influential background music of movies and television dramas. The psychologist Christopher Hsee has made important contributions in this area, summarized by Slovic. Sometimes ignored in academic discussions is that emotions can improve decision making, in particular where choice theory is not able to resolve a situation and where no apparently satisfactory rule of thumb is available, but, as is more often emphasized, they also can undermine rationality, impeding us from thinking clearly about the consequences of actions. The impact of many motivations can be overcome (or reduced) by incentives, often, even by close monitoring. The interaction between emotions and material self-interest can be seen in some of the so-called trust and ultimatum experiments (in which many participants elect not to accept what they regard as unfairly small amounts—even though, counter to the traditional affirmation that there is no such thing as a free lunch, the amounts are available without cost). The interaction between emotions and material self-interest also can be seen in a cost-benefit model of emotions and in an economic analysis of regret. Expressions of guilt, shame, revenge, contempt, hatred and indignation are often viewed later as having been counterproductive. The variety of emotions we have interact with each other and together with cognitive factors, produce behavior. Clearly, emotions can shape preferences and choices in certain contexts, particularly in the short run.

Some recent work of psychologists focuses on motivation and mood (both of which are influenced by perceived ability), and on the multidimensionality of emotions as well as on cognition. Psychologists attempt to provide a conceptual framework for understanding the importance of emotions (and visceral effects) in guiding judgments and decisions, which they refer to as the affect heuristic. This is especially important in dealing with personal attributes (in what they term, attributes substitution). Affective reactions to stimuli often occur first, automatically, subsequently orienting information processing and judgment. Some affect is present in all perceptions, but this may be truer for everyday matters than for most business, investment and government transactions. The utility we experience may be colored by feelings of affect that have become associated with certain past events, and contrast with a parallel rational process system involving decision theory. At the same time, it is doubtful that utility maximization (whether the maximization of profits, sales or of any other goals) is really what energizes human behavior in many circumstances. (It may be the ability to react rapidly, as Simon has suggested some biologists maintain.) In any event, affect conditions our preferences, which may help explain why our preferences are not always stable even in the short run (and this may be every bit as important as the now stressed differences in framing).

There is a strong relationship between images and decision making, and this is part of the explanation for the current emphasis on design and choice architecture. This relationship ranges from predictions of preferences for investing in new companies to predictions of the likelihood of adolescents taking part in health-threatening and health-enhancing behavior such as smoking and exercise. The precision of an affective impression makes a difference, as does the degree to which the decision involves a comparison. Proportions generally dominate actual numbers in guiding decisions, though if it comes to a matter of saving lives, experiments show that options worded in terms of the number of lives saved are generally regarded more than those that focus on the proportion of lives saved. Generally. In any event, warnings are more effective in vivid, affect–laden scenarios than when presented in terms of statistical frequencies.

People are often insensitive to probability data when the consequences of some options carry strong affective connotation, as with cancer through the 1950s and since, and risks such as those involving nuclear hazards and toxic chemicals. Activities associated with cancer are seen as riskier and more in need of public recognition than activities associated with less dreaded forms of illness, injury or death, even though the overall adverse consequences of the latter also may be quite high (perhaps even as high in the case of heart disease). In certain contexts (and this is one of the findings of the initial empirical work in Prospect Theory), alternatives with low probabilities can carry great weight, which seems to be important in explaining a decision maker's election of both gambling and insurance options, even at the same time. Judgments of risk and major benefits sometimes are negatively correlated and often this does not change much with the presentation of hard evidence to the contrary; in fact, with many innovative activities, the greater the perceived benefit, the lower the risk that is perceived. As a consequence of this and favorable affective associations, some activities to which people react favorably are perceived as having low risk even when this is patently not true. The impact of the availability heuristic may be due not just to the ease of recall, but to recall images that bring affect to the forefront. Willingness to pay for provision of a public good or a punitive damage award in a personal injury law suit may be influenced by emotional attitudes regarding those matters as well as by indicators of economic value.

Preliminary studies suggest that individuals with greater intelligence lean more towards cognitive than emotional solutions. Aside from the problems this sometimes causes (notably delay in making decisions), there are exceptions to it when powerful drives or emotions come into play. (Again, this qualified finding is part of the reason why traditional economists are so skeptical of behavioral economics and allied psychological analyses.) The tendency of greater intelligence to lead to cognitive approaches is influenced by individual experience and expertise, social, cultural and economic factors, but, unfortunately, the extent of the influence is not yet clear (which further raises the skepticism of traditional economists about applying behavioral economics).

Although mainstream economics long considered rational decision making as basically a cognitive process, and some of the initial contributions from psychology's behavioral decision analysis tended to reinforce that, it is now clear that emotional and even visceral factors can play a role in improving the rationality of decision making—as well as in undermining it, as had been emphasized previously. Visceral factors are essentially physiological and generally evolve without thinking about them. Emotional factors are more complex, and usually involve cognitive thought. Ascertaining exactly how the visceral and emotional factors influence decision making (and explaining the variations) remains very much a work in progress. In particular, more work is needed on the role of incentives in offsetting emotional and well as visceral factors.

Although dealt with under other topics, the matter of confidence levels also should be considered in discussing emotional factors. This is mainly a matter of overconfidence, but lack of confidence is sometimes also a factor. High levels of confidence can reflect some special skill or managerial capacity, but often overconfidence reflects other-than-rational factors. This is widely the case but can amusingly be seen in the famous Swedish example in which most drivers found in a hospital ward after an accident, characterized themselves as "above average drivers." Unfortunately, as noted before, and as economists Dubra and Benoit have tirelessly shown, many of the "proofs" of overconfidence are deficient.

12

STRATEGIC INTERACTION

In economics, both traditional and behavioral, the coverage of strategic interaction has been dominated by game theory and that literature is laid out in most microeconomics texts. This has proven useful in certain contexts, though perhaps less so than was originally anticipated. Behavioral economists have adapted the original format, developing a behavioral game theory.

Four major assumptions characterize standard game theory. The first is that people have correct mental representations of the relevant game. The second is that people have unbounded rationality. The third is that equilibrium positions are reached instantly (there is no learning). The fourth is that people are motivated purely by self-interest. Behavioral game theory, on the other hand, maintains, first, that the representations of the game be correct. Bounded rationality prevails in that there is incomplete information with a tendency to rely on factors such as mutually accepted focal points and mutually agreed-upon signaling, and that there are limits on the strategic thinking and backward induction capabilities of humans. Correlated rather than what is termed Nash equilibria are common (although some authorities are comfortable with Nash equilibria). Further, it is maintained that "noise"—irrelevant and unwanted information—may interfere with intended signals.

Third, equilibrium positions may change because learning (as revealed in games) takes place. (Actually, as noted above, traditional game theory now involves a form of learning.) Fourth, social preferences are involved (particularly given the real world reality of limitations on backward induction—the ability of individuals to reason from optimal end moves to prior optimal moves), and this also influences the selection of accepted focal points. Behavioral game theory has a sounder basis in psychology and is supported more often by experimental evidence, although little effort has been undertaken to incorporate material concerning the behavioral responses from real world actors that might emerge from interview-based studies.

An important qualification to the limited usefulness of game theory and the reticence of many of its practitioners to accept the findings of behavioral economics is noted at the end of this section.

There are other alternatives of strategic interaction, but it may be useful to outline basic considerations with respect to learning, a dynamic process that is usually assigned importance in economic analysis (certainly in strategic interaction), but which economists have yet to explain well—and that is particularly important for behavioral economics. Texts in behavioral economics consider four types of learning—reinforcement learning, belief learning, experience-weighted attraction learning, and rule learning. The first has not been well regarded since the 1960s, and the last three have emerged more in recent years, due to the contributions of behavioral game theorists. Although much of what economists have written about learning comes from the results of game theory experiments, what follows is taken from various papers of Simon, most written in collaboration with psychologists and represents the thinking of psychology as of the mid-to-late 1990s. It extends learning concepts beyond those relevant for game theory. A similar summary was published by this author in books in 1998 and 2008 and in an economics journal early in the 21st Century, the latter of which was included in a volume of articles on Simon, but this view has not been critically evaluated by economists. What follows is, perhaps unfortunately, the least accepted of the material in this presentation and the rest of Section 12 can be skipped by those who merely seek the gist of what behavioral economists have concluded, with the exception of the last paragraph, which does reflect an important new development, highly recognized and handsomely praised by the leaders in the economics profession.

Learning can be defined as the understanding gained, usually over a period of time that is retained long enough to lead to some change in behavior for the activities to which it applies. This definition would rule out lessons seemingly learned, perhaps even leading to satisfactory initial applications, but that are not subsequently applied in relevant real life situations. Most definitions of learning would not require that the changes in behavior be permanent, however. Langley and Simon have defined learning in complex systems as any process that modifies the system so as to improve, more or less irreversibly, its subsequent performance of the same task or similar tasks. Learning may change preferences, and may change the way in which processes are implemented. Learning may be reflected in innovations which have become an important topic in economic inquiry, especially by those who have been called neo-Schumpeterians, and appears to be important in many of the IT innovations of recent years.

In the basic economic model, there is perfect knowledge and perfect rationality so that there is really no role for learning. Economists have moved beyond that and have long acknowledged learning in a variety of ways, in particular, as a lagged reaction that improves the ability to achieve technical efficiency over time, or to advance beyond that and realize technological change. Mainstream economists have often referred to learning by doing—by producing, by exporting or by realizing some active experience—but the discipline of economics, which so emphasizes efficiency, has had little to say about how one can (or should) achieve or assess an efficient process of learning, particularly if the underlying conditions are changing, as they usually are. Nobel laureate Joseph Stiglitz has written of "learning to learn." An effort to integrate the analysis of learning into the general framework of economic analysis can be seen in Young Back Choi's observations that even the basic decision making process involves learning inasmuch as it reflects a successful search for a paradigm to cope with a situation that we could not make sense of before.

Even as economists find themselves grappling with the question of learning, most seem to ignore much of the work that is being done in psychology on the subject. To what extent can psychology help economics and finance to understand learning and make the appropriate assumptions about the matter?

Psychology offers half a dozen lines of thought on learning which can be categorized as:

- Stimulus and Response
- Cognitive Learning
- Social Learning
- Learning by Programmed Instruction
- Latent Learning
- Organizational Learning

Stimulus and Response. The classic studies in this area analyze simultaneous stimulus and response. The work in the middle of the twentieth century dealt with reinforcement (operant conditioning), which involved the use of repeated stimuli. The ensuing responses were characterized as instinctive. Skinner and his followers obtained results independent of the findings of physiological psychology or cognitive psychology. Also under the heading of Stimulus and Response has been the work in behavior modification, first with electric shock and, increasingly in recent decades, with drugs, as more and more problems have been analyzed in term of chemical imbalances. Many psychologists have adopted one or another of these stimulus response approaches. Very few economists have done so, the most notable exceptions being David Alhadeff in the early 1980's and recent work on animal behavior.

Cognitive Learning. Cognitive learning deals with insights, reasoning and imagination and emphasizes retrieval and extraction, association, repetition, recognition and the solution of problems. Some psychologists have pointed to the difficulties of learning, in particular the need for suitable feedback, and to the phenomenon of negative or incorrect learning. This might be considered in the light of some of the work of Mancur Olson and other economists who have maintained that institutions do not always improve in terms of their economic impact—contrary to what one might expect from a survival-of-the-rational-optimizer line of thinking).

While the early work in cognitive learning recalls the name of Piaget, and often difficult verbal constructs, a new tradition has been evolving. This has developed in part from work with computer simulations and computer tutor programs, from the use of visual imagery in thinking—from what psychologists refer to as connectionist learning schemes and adaptive productions systems and from various protocols including one in which individuals are asked to "think aloud" while they are solving problems—that is, they are asked not to "introspect" or "retrospect." This work dealt with at somewhat greater length below under the heading, The New Research in Cognitive Learning, is being used in the field of management science and seems to offer important applications for economics. (Psychologists state that connectionist learning schemes postulate networks that learn by changing the strengths of their interconnections in response to feedback.)

Social Learning. The term social learning refers to cognitive processes backed up by reinforcement. It has been broken down into direct learning, indirect learning, and imitation and emulation. One of the leading applications has been by those focused on marketing.

Learning by Programmed Instruction. Learning by Programmed Instruction draws on a variety of theories and received a great deal of attention in the mid 1960's. Although the results were less successful than expected, the programs have become more interactive, and have been greatly improved.

Latent Learning. This term refers to phenomena such as the learning of rats in a labyrinth and to unplanned (unpremeditated) learning that draws on early general education. An example of the role assigned to latent learning that draws on early general education can be seen in the conviction of some individuals and enterprises that a strong primary and secondary school (and now perhaps college) education that provides general tools, together with an inquiring frame of mind, are more important for success in business than training in specific skills or analytic tools. Bill Gates, Michael Dell and Steve Jobs may be examples of this, but Stephen Wozniak, Warren Buffet and Jamie Dimon, also examples of recent success in the economy, seem to be such counterexamples that the first group may just refer to exceptions.

Organizational Learning. Organization Learning has not received a great deal of attention from psychologists, but this neglect may be coming to an end as works in psychology have explained some of the central ideas of economic and business administration. A major text in the theoretical aspect of managerial economics emphasizing the importance of coordination internal to the enterprise, Milgrom and Roberts 1992, refers primarily to the importance of "routines," a concept introduced into the economics and management literature by Nelson and Winter in their seminal 1982 volume.

The New Research in Cognitive Learning. In 1975, Simon wrote that learning does not refer to a single, simple set of human cognitive processes and does not involve one kind of change, or a change in one component of the system. He offered eight considerations for researchers to bear in mind, particularly those dealing with the learning processes of students:

1. The kinds and degree of understanding that a student achieves in solving a task can have important consequences for his or her retention of skill and knowledge, ability to transfer that knowledge, and the speed and efficiency with which additional knowledge is acquired.
2. Understanding has many facets.
3. An important component of problem-solving skill lies in being able to recognize salient problem features rapidly and to associate promising solution steps with those features. (In a later study, Simon provides the example of a chess master being able to recall the position of pieces in well-defined game situations much better than the novice, but not being much better in recalling the position of randomly placed pieces.)
4. Limits of short-term memory may prevent application of a problem-solving method that is understood.
5. Understanding generally requires not only storage of adequate semantic information but also the availability of problem-solving schemata of a general and a specific character.

6. Syntactic may often be substituted for semantic processing and vice versa.
7. Understanding processes entails being able to construct representation of problem situations.
8. It is becoming increasingly possible to determine in detail what understanding any specific matter involves. Thus, it has become possible to write computer programs for solving problems and for acquiring new knowledge in a domain.

Research has been shifting back and forth between the attention given to performance and that given to learning processes. Research in cognitive learning has attempted, first, to understand human performance, how the human brain stores and processes various kinds of semantic representations and to incorporate that information into computer programs. Importance has been given to the recognition of patterns. A number of experiments in China have shown that students learned high school mathematics as well when they were presented with carefully chosen sequences of problems and were asked to work out the examples, as when they were first offered instruction on the basic principles involved. (This finding seems to lend support to the contention that educational institutions have determined their teaching methods by use of very rough rules of thumb, without any deep understanding of learning processes.) The students in the mathematics learning experiment acquired knowledge from examples in what is referred to as "productions," which are defined as sets of conditions leading to actions.

Initially, the students discovered conditions under which the actions were appropriate and then elaborated the conditions to increase the efficiency of their actions. Researchers do not appear to know how close the results of the traditional teaching methods or the approach using worked-out examples are to achieving the most efficient mathematics learning results. A similar comment can be made with respect to the experiments that move to "adaptive production programs"—systems that reprogram themselves (computer programs that learn by generating new instructions that are annexed to existing ones.) Among the other issues that arise are the respective roles of logical reasoning, on the one hand, and selective search processes (search algorithms) using mental methods in problem solving, on the other. Other concepts include what the psychologists have defined as procedural-ization, composition, and the building of efficient productions that recog-nize useful configurations. (Psychology provides precise definitions for all of these concepts.). Finally, experiments have supported the intuitive propo-sitions that the efficiency of learning mechanisms differs according to the learner's native abilities and prior learning experience.

Langley and Simon list the characteristics of a good explanation of learning to learn as involving a "set of invariants," but also as:

1. Explaining a variety of phenomena;
2. Being more basic than the phenomena it explains;
3. Being simpler than those phenomena; and
4. Being free of ad hoc components.

Two conclusions emerge. First, we are just beginning to understand the basic guidelines for improving the efficiency of learning. (Consider how long it has taken artificial intelligence to achieve what it stated de-cades ago that it would be able to do—not that I mean to belittle what has been accomplished.) We have no notion of how to maximize learning processes, and we are only beginning to develop reasonable guidelines for what Simon characterized as satisficing, though we do seem to have a better basis for avoiding learning disasters. Second, work in economics that attributes importance to learning is not even using available heuristics that might at least avoid serious error and perhaps facilitate satisficing. (If anyone doubts the next-to-last point, consider the experience of the period just before the financial and economic crisis that began in late 2007.)

Note that Colin Camerer concluded more than a decade ago that learn-ing is very difficult even in simple deterministic situations. He reports that even experts in various fields routinely violate rationality in their use of readily available information. (Recall the dramatic example revealed by the Allais experiments with leading economists in the early 1950s in which the latter literally dismissed the errors they had made.) Moreover, we do not seem to know how to design experiments or specify models capable of capturing the learning of individuals who have a great deal of tacit information that is not easily explicable.

Although a much better understanding of learning is critical to good economic analysis, from the point of view of most economists, psychology offers too many explanations. In any event, considering cognitive psychology alone, while economics is devoting a great deal of attention to the findings of this subfield in the area of decision making, our discipline continues to ignore the improved new heuristics on cognitive learning.

Sociology may offer some assistance at the organizational level. A disconcerting phenomenon is that even if people appear to learn, they do not always apply that learning beyond the immediately subsequent period. Furthermore, many decisions are made too infrequently to provide a good basis for learning, or if made more often, do not facilitate a quality of feedback that is conducive to learning. At least some of the learning required for economic and financial decision making requires much more than what is needed for the propositions about secondary school mathematics (for which the basic solutions are well known). Finally, psychologists have shown that individuals' confidence tends to increase with experience, regardless of the character and quality of the judgments made with that experience.

As indicated above, traditional game theory or rather, a modification of it (that some traditional game theorists do not accept), has proven useful in improving the initial selection in markets in which the use of prices is prohibited or limited and in which the matching process between those involved in supply and in demand requires assistance. Alvin Roth, a recent co-winner of the Nobel Prize in economics, has written *Who Gets What – and Why* (Boston and New York, 2015; Eamon Dolan—Houghton Mifflin Harcourt), outlining his and his colleagues' successful efforts in using game theory and in developing algorithms to allocate kidney transplants, to select schools for college students, and to determine the placement of medical school graduates and judicial clerks. The approach outlined accepts at least some behavioral economics and considers second and other lesser choices as well as what is most sought. It coincides with behavioral game theory in giving attention to signaling. It does not extend to decision making beyond the initial phase, however, and it does not incorporate what psychology indicates about learning—but it does improve the initial matching of supply and demand in comparison to what prevailed before in such non-price areas. Whether the outcomes might be better if account were taken of learning as described by psychology or not, whether the outcomes might be still better if account were taken of the responses in-depth interviews of those involved in the supply and demand side, and whether both might enable good results beyond the initial stage of matching is a matter of speculation. (It is assumed that the additional costs incurred of obtaining any such improved results would be less than the benefits obtained.) What no is longer a matter of speculation, though, is that a form of behavioral game theory can improve initial stage matching and is being used for that purpose.

13

NEUROECONOMICS

Neuroeconomics, a mix of neurology and economics, has been cited as underlying all behavioral economics by an increasing number of behavioral economists but put aside by others as not yet having added to what behavioral economics has to offer. It represents an effort to locate and measure the utility of certain results and has been advanced by the use of position emission tomography (PET), magnetic resonance imaging (fMRI), and transcranial magnetic stimulation (TMS), primarily fMRI, which focuses on blood flows. (PET detects changes in neurotransmitter release.) It is well to keep the following conclusions in mind:

1. The brain is composed of many components and systems and these interact in leading to our decision making;
2. Different stages of decision making recruit different components of the brain;
3. The brain responds differently during anticipation of incentives than in response to incentive outcomes, an indication of what has been termed reference dependence; and
4. The processing of gains does not appear to be simply the opposite of the processing of losses.

Neuroeconomics has identified and better explained the locus of various aspects of decision making, but it has not yet been able to indicate what precisely needs to be done to alter outcomes. If the brain is inclined to perform in a particular manner in given circumstances, what type and level of incentives are required to lead to certain desired changes? Some types and level of incentives might achieve that but neuroeconomics is not at the stage of being able to answer that critical question, and we do not know if it ever will be.

14

ALTRUISM, JUSTICE, SOCIAL NORMS AND INSTITUTIONS

The model of traditional economic analysis is one in which the basic motivation is self-interest. Social norms and issues of justice do not intervene, and as for institutions, they are minimal, only those that are required for an economic system such as capitalism to function (the concept of the night watchman). That is a model, however, it is not the real world.

In the real world, altruism, justice, social norms and institutions play a role, or may do so. People volunteer, and not only after they retire from remunerative employment. Contributions are made to charity (particularly large ones after major disasters), and not only for tax deductions (indeed, some of the largest contributions in the United States relative to incomes were made before the possibility of tax deductions came into play), tips are left for waiters even in circumstances unlikely to be repeated, citizens vote even when not compelled by law and though there may not be any apparent economic return, some employees work harder and longer than they really need to for the compensation they earn (while it is true that others are free riders as traditional economics assumes is likely to often be the case), companies volunteer to maintain stretches of public highway, enlightened selfishness if not quite altruism is extended in some places of employment by employees unlikely to rise much if at all in rank, trust is often extended in a wide variety of situations, and so on. More than strict self-interest is often at play, and the extension is not exclusively to family and friends. Moreover, punishments are sometimes meted out and even at a cost to those who do the punishing, standards are established which, while apparently in the public interest, often lead to what has been termed moral hazard (with repetitions of a problem likely to be fostered), and certain individuals and groups are treated in a manner that is not in the best economic interest of those treating them unfairly or the larger society. And there is deception, cheating and rank opportunism—along with a signaling of intentions that reduces the advantage that market transactions would enable, but perhaps that may reflect expected reciprocity in some cases.

Economists have begun to write more about these matters in recent years, and those efforts are part of what is involved in behavioral economics. This type of response was given a new emphasis with the creation of ultimatum, dictator and trust games in which participants have shown their unwillingness to accept what they regard as unfair shares, even though they have not had to pay for them, and where the result has been influenced by the trust accorded to those offering the amounts in question. The desirability of fairness is now well recognized, but the standard of what is fair often varies between (and even within) communities and societies as well as over time, and almost always varies according to circumstances. Tipping a cab driver is expected in large cities but not in many smaller communities. Purchasing shares in a company with an outstanding future is generally well regarded (even where it goes against rational diversification), but raising prices after a destructive hurricane is not. And arriving at 2 PM for a scheduled contract signing may be essential on Wall Street, or expected in the case of a 6 PM cocktail reception, but such timely behavior is not even expected in many developing societies. Picking up a ten dollar bill left on the sidewalk may always make good sense, but the ultimatum and dictator games economists have revealed that a very small division of unexpected and unearned gains is usually not regarded as fair and not accepted. See Shiller's *Irrational Exuberance* for a forceful presentation on the role of social factors in influencing financial transactions.

Social preferences and the institutions that reflect them differ between communities, and they can change over time. Indeed, they can vary even in short time frames with new exposure, learning and even more frequent repetition of events that were previously regarded as infrequent. Some environments foster more cooperation or consideration than others, and, indeed, some such inclinations may have an evolutionary explanation. Trust matters, as does anonymity, and the expectation of reciprocity. Moreover, the size of stakes and level of economic opportunity can as well. One's personal wealth may enter, as also may the level of competition, the amount of information that is available and the means of dealing with it. So, too, may any record of past intentions and the cost of punishment. Gender matters, at least in some situations (seen not only in the disparity in pay between the sexes, but also in the differences in attitudes towards investment—in which women have been shown to be more conservative and men more inclined towards taking on risk), as may age and the culture one comes from. One text defines social norms as behavioral regularities and socially shared beliefs regarding how one ought to behave, both of which are enforced by social sanctions (which might be defined as institutional understandings). To the winner go the spoils, it is often proclaimed, but economist Mancur Olson explained why institutionally ossified World War II victor Britain lost ground for several decades as it allowed in-groups to continue with earlier privileged positions that once may have contributed to national welfare and certainly to societal notions of fairness but no longer did, while defeated and institutionally much altered Japan gained in part precisely because of the elimination of former institutional privilege.

15

HAPPINESS

It is a legitimate question whether economics—even behavioral economics—ought to be focused on assessments that go beyond strictly economic considerations. While one may note the psychological content of economic decision making, as behavioral economics does, it is quite another matter to assess the welfare or "happiness" implications of the resulting economic outcomes. At the same time, it must be conceded that welfare has been a concern of some economists at least since the turn of the 20th Century with the development of welfare economics and perhaps since the writings of Malthus in the early 19th Century.

Happiness involves comparisons of the perceived well-being of the members of a community over time even as some people in the community may be less well-off while others are better off. Wilkinson and Klaes' *An Introduction to Behavioral Economics* (London and New York, 2014; Routledge) concludes, as have many economists, that happiness has increased over several decades. The position of this writer is that economics offers little basis for such a conclusion.

Let us proceed with the majority analysis, though.

To begin with, there is a general inclination and considerable empirical work supporting the conclusion that while higher levels of income lead to greater happiness at first, this does not continue *ad infinitum*. Further, all agree that happiness and unhappiness are not symmetrical reflections of gains and losses. It is acknowledged, moreover, that happiness is a subjective category, compared to such matters as costs, individual income levels, or GDP.

The Wilkinson and Klaes text characterize happiness as a dispositional trait, rather than a reaction to external events. No dissent there though it is not clear that economics has much to offer in measuring and evaluating dispositional traits.

Analysts of happiness and human welfare conclude that people adapt to repeated experiences of a given type of event, putting aside disagreeable and unsuccessful experiences (for the most part) if they are successful, and anticipating at least as much in the future as in the past. Experience becomes a reference point to which new experiences and anticipated experiences are compared. Agreed, but there are too many exceptions to generalize and, in any event, it is not clear how exactly this contributes to an evaluation of happiness.

Wilkinson and Klaes conclude that happiness results more from pursuing a goal than from attaining it. Psychologists certainly have been asserting this, but there may be many exceptions. Even if it is the case generally, and there is some truth in it, ask the former Japanese company Vice President who retired on a sizable pension at age 55 if he is happier now than before, given that he has no chance of becoming CEO of his company which he long sought, but he can sleep better at night and has a statistically better chance of living past age 65. And what of the great majority of Silicon Valley entrepreneurs who do not become millionaires despite long hours of sacrifice and higher rates of drug abuse and divorce than in the country as a whole—or for most of us who do not attain the ambitious goals we once held?

The authors of the Wilkinson and Klaes text observe that people possess a psychologically immune system that speeds recovery from negative emotional events. This is true on average (though not for all, with some indeed becoming severally damaged mentally, and consider, in any event, the problem of intra-personal evaluations). In any event, not becoming depressed is not the same as being more content than before.

Some happiness authors state that people reduce the emotional power of events by coming to make them seem ordinary and predictable, even explainable. This may be true on average, but even for those who succeed in doing this, does it mean that they are happier than before? Again, the task of intra-personal comparison may be insurmountable.

Some researchers base their models in part on evolutionary biology and on the assumption that happy individuals are more likely to breed successfully. The first part of the sentence certainly is relevant, but as for the second part, one would have to wonder if happiness is what best explains the ability to survive. Also, one would have to conclude that Latin Americans, with a much reduced rate of birth, are much less happy than 50 years ago—which would seem to go against the conclusions of some studies.

Wilkinson and Klaes note several limitations of pursuing (even) the hedonic aspects of happiness:

1. There are limits to hedonic happiness and to our ability to measure happiness accurately.
2. There are adverse effects of hedonic introspection on well-being.
3. There are self-defeating aspects of happiness seeking, notably that people have faulty theories of happiness, that happiness-seeking may lead to a loss of the appreciation of the intrinsic value of activities, and that increased monitoring of happiness may interfere with happiness itself.

One of the contributions of the Cartwright text is presentation of the issues raised by Kahneman concerning what exactly is meant by utility—whether we have in mind the utility that is experienced (and, if so, just when), that which is remembered, or that which is anticipated.

16

MAJOR APPLICATIONS: BEHAVIORAL FINANCE, PUBLIC FINANCE AND "NUDGING"

Economists were reticent to accept a behavioral approach to economic topics until the mid-1990s (though Gary Becker and his followers did take the view that virtually all phenomena could be explained by traditional economic considerations) and, indeed, there is still negligible behavioral analysis in a number of fields. This section considers several areas where major applications have been made. The most numerous have been in behavioral finance. The second is more mainstream public finance, where three economists have prepared a very useful survey, followed by an even more general application of behavioral economics to the design of economic policy. A third is the area of nudging, paternal libertarianism, in which the emerging contributions have included a popular book coauthored by a leading behavioral economist and an eminent lawyer who helped establish what is known as behavioral law, and who held a position implementing federal laws and regulations in the United States for several years. Finally, at long last, behavioral economics is beginning to influence the field of development economics (although many in the social sciences have been critical of the limited approach of economics for a hundred years or more).

In the mid-1990s most texts on finance scarcely mentioned behavioral finance. The field was celebrating extraordinary years of financial gain and the naming of several Nobel Prize laureates who contributed to financial economics. Efficient markets were proclaimed in the strongest terms, rationality was the byword and new mechanisms were innovated to take advantage of all of this by mathematicians and mathematically more capable economists. Some authors found that studies raising doubts received a better response from journal reviewers if they did not cite psychologists whose experimental work seemed to underlie the emerging wave of events. Several analyses that pointed to anomalies were rejected by leading journals *because* they contradicted the basic principles of rationality. Even as this was happening, a maverick mathematician produced works dissenting from the traditional focus and orientation of economists, and some econometricians raised questions about the number of years on which the conclusions of market growth and market efficiency were based. An increasing number of anomalies were being documented with the journals of finance among those leading the way.

In 1981 Robert Shiller documented that the volatility in the level of real stock prices on the New York Stock Exchange greatly exceeded what might be expected from changes in the level of the real value of dividends, the latter of which presumably constituted the leading reason for purchasing stock shares (and he showed in the 1981 and subsequent publications that the stock volatility was not in response to anticipated movements in dividends). This came on top of the 1979 *Econometrica* article of Kahneman and Tversky presenting a behavioral alternative to the expected utility standard as the explanation of decision making. Shiller characterized the stock market as highly overvalued as early as 1995 and continued to do so up until 2000-2001 when the market indeed declined sharply; later, he warned of a housing bubble and ensuing economic collapse in the period just prior to the 2007-2009 crisis. While few experts or practitioners supported those views, the increasing interest of financial academics and practitioners in applications of behavioral economics coincided with the interests of an appreciable number of practitioners who were skeptical of the efficient markets hypothesis and sought a more active role in their field. An increasing number of academics who had been influenced by the emerging behavioral decision theory undertook studies of market anomalies.

The best way to view the attention that behavioral economics has received in finance is to note that in addition to several behavioral finance surveys (cited in the Shiller and Thaler volumes), not only is there much more on behavioral finance in finance texts than in the mid-1990s, but there are now also texts in behavioral finance.

Lucy Ackert and Richard Deaves co-authored one of the best known recent texts in behavioral finance. It begins with two chapters on the foundations of finance—expected utility theory, asset pricing, market efficiency and what economists call agency relationships. This is followed by a chapter on Prospect Theory, framing and mental accounting. Chapter 4 concerns challenges to market efficiency, noise trading, and limits to arbitrage, incorporating a number of the empirical findings from the behavioral finance literature. The first part of the chapter deals with seemingly irrational lagged reactions to earnings announcements, what have been termed small-firm effects, value vs. growth and momentum investing, and the investment reversal phenomenon (whereby stocks that are "winners" in a period of years subsequently do not fare as well in the period ahead as those which were "losers"). The second part includes material on social factors but emphasizes limits to arbitrage—which traditional economic theory ignored (or presumably, considered only temporary)—and inefficiencies in pricing. Chapters 5-7 cover heuristics and biases, overconfidence and emotions.

Chapters 8-10 deal with investment behavior. Chapter 8, Familiarity, Availability and Home bias, covers studies that reflect several heuristics, and considers trend following, short vs. long term investments and the difference between good companies and good investments. Chapter 9 discusses the role of overconfidence. Chapter 10, Individual Investors and the Force of Emotion, deals with a wide range of topics including happiness. Attention is given to behavioral differences that may arise in dealing with "house money" and with alternative explanations of what has been called the disposition effect (whereby it is maintained that stocks that have gained are sold too soon and those that have lost value are held for too long). Chapters 11 and 12 deal with social forces and include coverage of the fairness studies, and also the collapse of Enron. Chapters 13 and 14 consider behavioral explanations for the anomalies of individual decision making, beginning with the literature concerning earnings announcements and the value vs. growth stocks debate. Included is a discussion of the alternative efforts to deal with the momentum investing and the investment reversal phenomenon. The insufficiently explained equity puzzle (whereby stocks earn a premium over bonds that exceeds their long term risk), bubbles and stock market volatility also are considered.

The remainder of the text includes applications of behavioral analysis to corporations, debiasing, behavioral investing and neurofinance.

For an account—a riveting account—of the role of behavioral finance considerations in helping to explain recent (and not-so-recent) economic crises, see Andrew Palmer's chapter, From Breakdown to Meltdown, in the 2015 volume, *Smart Money* (New York, Basic Books).

While most courses in economics continue to make little mention of behavioral anomalies and assumptions, a rather different approach can be found in *Policy and Choice. Public Finance Though the Lens of Behavioral Economics*, by William Congdon, Jeffrey Kling and Sendhil Mullainathan. *Policy and Choice* begins with a number of general considerations, noting, for example, that psychological costs and benefits may differ from economic ones. Humans are characterized by imperfect optimization, bounded self-control, and preferences that differ from those assumed by traditional theory, it is maintained. There are unintended behavioral responses, incentives influenced by lack of willpower, procrastination, temptation and other factors such as context, an individual's state, emotional considerations, and addiction. Problems arise due to limits in the "attraction" of different categories of information, limits in human computational capacity and reasoning that is influenced by motivational considerations. A chapter follows that deals with diagnosing policy problems, assessing policy alternatives and prescribing policy responses. Part II deals with how behavioral economics might contribute to economists' concerns about asymmetric information, and with externalities and public goods, poverty and inequality and taxation and revenue. Brigitte Madrian's piece, Applying Insights from Behavioral Economics to Policy Design, used in her course at Harvard's Kennedy School, builds on the Congdon, Kling and Mullainathan paper, providing guidelines to economic policy design generally, and deals with deviations from optimality that are due to such matters as location, lack of will power, and other-than-economic recognition rather than the economist's traditional focus on marginal costs and benefits.

The "nudging" literature completes the step of transforming behavioral economics from a passive indication of how economic actors make decisions to a more normative effort to get individuals and other economic entities to alter their decision making to ways more in line with their own interests (which, in at least some cases, may move them towards optimization in terms of society's objectives). The approach appears to have begun with Thaler and Shlomo Bernartzi's successful efforts to have corporations induce employees to save more, and reached its high point with publication of *Nudge* by Thaler and Cass Sunstein (New Haven, 2008; Yale University Press). The approach, referred to as paternal liberalism, indicates how governments as well as private entities can induce individuals and others to change their decision making along the lines of their own interests in response to new incentives. A major question, emphasized by the Congdon et al. and Madrian contributions, is whether the default or other nudging options that happen to be selected, while representing improvements, are necessarily the most efficient mechanisms for getting individuals to make decisions that are in their own or in society's interest.

Finally, after a long history of avoiding other than traditional orientations, the development finance community is now incorporating more behavioral economics into its efforts, seen, most recently in the 2015 Word Bank Development Report, *Mind Society and Behavior.*

www.ingramcontent.com/pod-product-compliance
Lightning Source LLC
Chambersburg PA
CBHW050603280326
41933CB00011B/1964